SLEEPTALKING

SLEEPTALKING

ANTONIO ADDESSI

REBEL SATORI PRESS
NEW ORLEANS

Published in the United States of America and United Kingdom by
Rebel Satori Press
www.rebelsatoripress.com

Paperback ISBN: 978-1-60864-200-7
ebook ISBN: 978-1-60864-215-1
Library of Congress Control Number: 2022935223

Contents

Childhood

I was born in the back of a Buick LeSabre two months
too early during the same snow storm that caught
Kentucky by surprise sending my dad to a business
trip that only he knew the location of and no one not
even the father of our church knew where to find him
or if they would have a telephone that would reach which
is funny because the telephone in our house reached the floor
and slung clear around the corner to the rocking chair mom
would sit in breast feeding my sister in a storm that I would
remember being the only storm that scared my mother
into thinking freezing was a possibility when the pipes
froze and the basement filled like the Titanic and Leo
wasn't there to guide you up the stairs and the baseboard
heat would die with the electrical lines, the fire in the fireplace
would keep half the house in motion while the other slept
in a Sargasso gyre round the lakes and ponds that were
fished in the winter and boiled in the summer till they
dried up like clay pots filled with shrimp paste the old
women would scoop out and peel over their breasts humming
songs I knew the chorus to but not the solos and would
definitely not sing with the girls or play baseball with the
other boys instead I'd play mermaid diving to the dark
side of the lakebed where the silt would be ripe for the
throwing out onto the fly caked shore on which it would
attract everything but humans which was good for people
like me that wanted to lay alone letting the clay crack
open on my skin filling my belly with lake water.

Lovesick

adjective
1. languishing with love: YEARNING // a lovesick suitor
2. expressing a lover's longing

real love left the oceans for land thirty some odd years ago
real love pulled in her gills and pushed out lungs
real love cried salts and
real love wept into their coffee
real love sprouted hairs not thistle scales
real love met the stratosphere in a rocket ship
real love pierced the sky and beyond
real love smells of cigarette butts and palm oil

real love is sharing a space suit
real love should've used the bathroom before we descended
real love told your parents I was a woman
real love is showing but not pregnant maybe
real love can have a baby if I really try pull my gills in and shed my
            heart screaming
real love real love into the ceiling fan

real love pulls into the new epoch
real love puts the car on cruise control and pees into a gatorade bottle
real love is watering yourself
real love cuts the crust off into the sink
real love is tattoos on the linoleum
real love is watching you type in your dreams it's a

real love letter to me it's a touch screen in a laboratory
real love punch the code in

real love lets the mice out into your pocket
real love fill your pockets with sunflower seeds
real love loosens the bricks under the neighbors porch
real love lets you take me on the wharf wind and all
real love hikes up my underwear if I have them or rip them off in the
        name of
real love they're cheap and so is
real love you say is someone who'll chew your gum for you
real love makes your immune system bounce back
real love makes milk till there's nothing new

real love sees the baby take the wheel saying jesus take the wheel
real love lets me cut his hair and he cuts mine and
real love pulls me close in the park then lets me
real love be the little spoon all night dreaming
real love is seeing my name on the stern of your boat

Ragman

A Ragman's tiny suit of armor sitting there
not moving. A sliver of whale bone, once
part of a tussled breathing growing thing
now, a thatched roof bound to the rib cage.

He tells us that being bad is all about temper-
ment about bellyaching till the seams burst.
A wildfire starts near the woods we're camping
in but no one can smell the smoke except me.

I'm in my tent with the tentpoles bent round
me holding up the sky which is sad because
there isn't enough smog to make the sunset
memorable but there is a whole lot of talking

going on. Everyone is making sure that their
mates are home tucked in a log or high in
the fir trees that sound like highway grass as
we drift by in a rented truck. They wave at me

I don't have the courage to respond I just look
up while eating at my knuckle. A Ragman sits in
his tiny suit of armor sipping water from his
hands. Those hands are growing into me now

changing the way I walk, my reaction time
slows. He starts his story the same way he
always does. The man turns over in his sleep

4

his shoulders become the mountains. The sun

somehow knows what Ragman is going to say
and do. The leaves on the trees stay where
they are listening, waiting for their cue
to take that first breath.

Yams

I don't want this body
you say this with your
hips pushed out and your hands wrapped round
                    your waist. It's not the right size
                        the layout's all wrong
how can I breastfeed with yams?
I look down
where I wish breasts were but aren't
and pick up the vase on the table

                    I could turn it into firecrackers
                    the neighbors would think things
                    we could also take our clothes off
and draw circles like the doctors do

I take your yams in my hands and imagine
the skin all pulled back—they'd be steamy orange

the flowers in the vase shake as you walk the runner
toward the table

            if I cut them off would you leave?
            you say this with the letter opener in your hand

                    —I see your breasts on the floor one
                    has rolled under the duster and the
                    other sits there all cracked open sweet
            could the doctor put them back on?

I ask this with my hands where my breasts should be

you wouldn't cut them off I say
you'd have to buy all new tops
your carbon footprint

I want your body
you say this while pulling me into the bathroom
you have my body its yours
I pull my laundry underwear to the floor
you draw all over me in felt
rings round my belly button and the scar on my butt cheek
I stand there in the mirror all marked up and edited

I wouldn't change a thing
but I'd change for you
Is that love? I'm too afraid to ask
what's that smell?
the yams!
—you say this as you run to the stove
your breasts out of your apron

I love a scorched yam and I love you
I don't say this but I will someday

a solar flare at the edge of the galaxy 2.5 million years ago

At eleven I awoke thinking it was half past midnight.

I didn't have pubes but I had a new pair of converse and

a tootsie roll bank full of change. Ragman sits in his little

suit of something saying put your tongue to the nine volt.

I do and it feels wonderful. nine years later—

there's a nightclub filled city in view and six thousand miles

away a gap-toothed me takes off in a rocket ship toward

you as you say take it off like a costume in a small changing room

turn to me—Ragman tells me to pose before my eyes meet yours.

I do and it feels wonderful. I put the nine volt to my tongue.

the fizz is buzzing on my pallet and I can't stand in the rain anymore. these paper shoes are killing me; all pulp and sulfur.

I look up and the sun pelts me. mouth of iron. veins of copper.

I cross the street on the hottest day of March. Ragman tells me to look
    both ways.

I don't and it feels wonderful. You give me your hand and I take it.

garlic roaster

you told me there was love in the room
in the dining room and the kitchen
in the living room where we all fold our
feet and sing.   you told me there's
love in the hall closet
it's small but so are we and when we
get scared we can remember this moment
the moment where we became friends
where we   take a slow sip
and wait   for it
to happen.   I'm still waiting
waiting
for your feet   to patter up the stairs
waiting for you to step on the stage and
show me a love song   or that
glinting tooth   they don't see it
but I do   and when I say I miss
you, I say   missing you is what
gets me through the threshold of the
kitchen or the   dining room and I
step out and read a poem   cause
no one else will
they're too afraid or   they'll go next
they'll go to the head first   a long
piss onto or around the bowl   nothing
more   so I read   a poem
to you   and you alone a poem
about   the first time we met

I went   for a beer   nothing more
and there sat two gorgeous humans in a
kitchen
stacked there in the corner we connected
on garlic   and how and when
to roast   it.

old iron sides

she is
most days
a ship armed to the chin
cannons at her sides
her mast a sea of kelp and urchin

melting down my iron sides
for ammunition
she pours me
hot and slick
into molds I want to fit
but can't

what does her
naked belly show to sea's floor?

I want to see
I rubber my neck to her sides

only to take in salty sick
and the brim of her
matted cap

I pretend I am inside her—
below deck
she aches with barrels of cider
churning into
drink

to feed her crew
I want to be that crew
get paid little to feed her fuel
to work the nights
as the sea works her over
pandering toward open casks of
sea here
inlet there
till we drop anchor

Crawlspace

I take in a deep breath of what he says:
lying there for so long the man's shoulders
sprout leaves and tiny buds appear—

the mountains here are no longer naked
fifty years of growing   pushing up
holding together taking in and we

          hold
            up the sky

            Ragman doesn't look up from
the whale bone he's carving

                    I ask him if
the tide comes back   he doesn't answer he
          fixes on something past the dark I wonder
if you can hear it—

        the basement fills from the knees up

it's water it's clumps of fur raccoon pancake
thread and I feel my necktie legs loosen off
the ground

          I hear Ragman before the water
fills my ears: Changelings like us need a dark
place to call into

there's silt between my toes
my leggings are torn where the air feels
fresh I can see skin I tie myself into a half-
      windsor   it's morning.

orion's belting

you let me live in these arms
till the soda fizz tickles twisting
door frame you part I open into
quiet into the main squeeze
pushing forget-me-nots in a torn
t-shirt in the quotes hanging singing
call a friend! call that one million
standing in the butter saying
oats are better than barley
you can't afford sitting in the
quiet of our home

posing for you for the kelp forest
posing in the nude hurting pose
till you sing it open to a deranged
audience into the nothing letting go
oh babe! you with your song and spirit

I paint in the nude finding the right
light till it's what you've been
looking for tearing my skin from bone
my frontal lobe sits on the stoop
we sit on two teas soaked in the Hudson
soaked in the tannin stain my teeth
a breath labored me into the arm song
you play I pray the nightlights into dance

fish in the creel

At the end of summer we had a party for you
do you remember why you didn't show?
You'd been fishing in central park again
with your rod and your tackle box.
You told me you'd use the flies I tied
the ones I made to look like june bugs.
You said they were the most cunning things
you'd seen, that they'd put fish in the creel.
I had no idea what a creel was and I
didn't care. I just knew we'd be eating
fish for dinner and maybe after we ate
you'd show me your lucky tooth collection.

When you left the apartment I got the neighbors
to come over and made your favorites—lime jello
and ants-on-a-log. I waited about three hours, the sun
had gone and the neighbors too. That's when
I heard the phone ring. It was the police. They'd
found you in the Harlem Meer. You'd caught
the big one they said, you'd hooked a willow and
sank thigh deep into the muck. They hung up
when I asked if they'd bring you home.
It was late and I had my rollers in.

I hosed you off in the alley. No fish for dinner
instead we boiled your boot strings. You said
when you were flopping in the Meer you thought
a lot about my recipe for bran muffins and

where I got the hair to tie those flies. I couldn't
bring myself to tell you that hair was mine
that they may have looked like june bugs but
they were tiny red-eyed me's destined for
a mouth or three.

All My Wives

out of all my wives
        I know you'll be the best
your baleen mustache
        and the way you fix your hair
I don't even care that you own a taxidermy arctic fox
        she's cute and so is your accent

out of all my wives
        you're the one I want to tell my dreams to
right as I wake up—followed by you flossing my teeth
this can't be your first rodeo either
        veneers this great are only made in Cuba

out of all my wives
        I think you're the only one I won't be jealous of
        you should have a bull rider take you dancing
while I watch and take photos
        (I will edit myself into these photos
        at a later date)

out of all my wives
        I'll wait to eat you till the very end
        your toffee hair and saltwater taffy tube socks
you'll come into my life the way you left
        on roller skates in my brother's football jersey
me—I'll be in my best leotard stretching to the oldies.

honey dew

My ex-wife and I were still husband and wife
when she asked me to stop bringing rent boys
home. She said they didn't agree with the sheets
or the upholstery. I asked her to write this down
because I didn't want to forget. I wanted to show
her that I didn't pay for their company they were
my friends.

She stopped speaking to me. The upholstery
changed and so did our sleeping arrangements.
Why was she so angry? I was ok with her sleeping
with the pool boy. I had slept with him too. He
can ball a melon in under a minute and even
complimented my gusto.

II

A pool filled with water   eyes closed
                    arms stretched
calling out   echos   the slip
            we loved that game
        played it in bed after I turned out the light
                    you let me win.

III

When my ex-husband and I were still married
he found me in bed with the pool boy. He finished

cleaning the pool and I found myself beside it after
finishing watching the Young and the Restless. Out
of all the pool boys he was the gentlest. Hands that
held up melons to test if they were ripe rung me
like a towel onto the bedsheets.

He found us by way of his motion detecting camera
and he wasn't alone, his fans were watching. In my
first and last performance I was seen galloping into
sunrise, reverse cowgirl by 120,000 OnlyFans
subscribers. I screamed Marco and he,
he out of habit with his stupid game said Polo
from the closet where he's sat his whole life.

yardglobe

once in the back of a moving car looking
out you told me the earth was evil that it
didn't need us to grieve for it but let it go
the self it created created us and we are not
and never have been good.
                    the sky opens for a second
                              it was like I was
staring into one of those lawn globes the ones
old people buy and place in their yard to highlight
the summer only to mow around it watching
themselves in oval blues and purple.
                    a malignant tumor grows
                         the night swept past us in
that car but I don't remember ever leaving it
or going to bed but what I do remember is the
way your face tensed and your eyes never
left the window they stared out wishing for
something no one else had the answer to.
                    you take a photo of me eating
                              sometimes I lay
awake at night listening to you talk listening to
you sleeptalking to dreamme as your eyes flicker and I
wait for you to respond to those unanswered questions
you never do you tell me in the mornings that you were
waiting in line all night waiting in the grocery or for
the ferris wheel at Coney Island.
                    bathwater soaks the mattress
                         logic tells me to run during times of stress tells

me to find the nearest exit only this time the door
like the entrance to my building is sliding and takes
a minute to know I'm there there there you say you
say it's not all bad and I ask what isn't all bad and
you say us as you pull a piece of lint off my shirtsleeve.
        the tired sweater unravels

Mange

it's Prague in autumn
no, it's New York—
Ragman is so far from home   he's pinching a penny between two
                                                fingers   his coat looks like it
                                                has scabies   like
          that dog
                              we found at the bottom of
          cavagrande—
                    the itch comes and so does
                                                                              a
          taxi
                                                  Ragman tells me—
          take it
                              he says that the moon is in Libra
                    that so many men like me are out
                              I want to be like other people so bad
          so
                                        I look at my reflection in the
          window & practice my smile   it looks
          good   maybe someone will hold my hand tonight
          maybe   someone will use my real name

the taxi settles in the district
                              in a disco that opens   with cello lined walls
              I wanted to play the cello when I was
young but   my chicken wings
                                        couldn't prop up a bass or a
          baseball bat

I could float in the pool   swim round

I tread thru the crowd standing on my   tip toes for air   I can/could
dance once   I took classes   wanted to be held by all the
        guys
        lift me up so I can see   tried to tuck myself into a leotard
          hoped the other   boys would
        want to tuck there hands round my waist
                                        I don't weigh much
my chicken wings would flap   my grin—probably
        shit eating

                    it's biodome ballstick hot   I think
        about the warning signs of a stroke·   the smell of
                an electrical fire burning toast
        I wait and there's nothing
                something tells me layers need to be shed. I pepper
        grind out of my coat
& into a booth
                three men fold me into the mix   mix me a drink not
        asking to mix saliva but I let them   it tastes like burnt
        coffee and pop rocks

I won't be scared this time
        let my plus-fours to the ground
                    Ragman sits in the window
        watching me
wiggle out of my skivvies   kick them off into a

friendly face
        the night snowballs into polaroids   & gin ruins

            until the sky goes pastel

                    my ratty coat & I watching the
sunrise

from Roosevelt Island

Quatrains in Sarajevo

Night and she is breathing through an iron lung
an iron clad contraption in unison—hear the in-out
in-out starting midsection   where the city pinches
where the energy the synergy bottlenecks to merge

out comes a bouncing baby in comes a glimpse into
past participles spoken by a she in historic settings
telling us it's better if we keep our coats on
that being here is all about the eyes less about body

she tumbles next up granite staircases littered with
holes   some patched patchy so roomy so
empty this room all snakes and children in blankets
like pythons wrapped tight coil gripping canvas

as I wonder where all that river water comes from
where it's going and does it take its time—sip a short
coffee and read the funnies does it lean in to tell the
best part of the conversation to me and me alone?

does it wash down from the mountains? It has to!
I think it must! It comes from the clouds butting up
rubbing up against the cliffs all shoulders and elbows
through the crowd all "hey that's my seat you're in."

oh the rush! drink it up—the coldest water in a snug
town drink it up—the coiled blanket of a stomach
full of ink and stationary of plans for letters to write

home to never send to keep for ourselves in a tin.

Hostile Takeover

It's done, I've held up my end of the bargain.
I say this with the lampshade over my head

holding the lightbulb between the webs of
my toes. she'll never bother you again. she

as in she and I as in I like that you think I
have control over what another person does.

I can't see you for the lampshade crowds
my view. there is a siren outside and I hope

it's for me. I wait for the downstairs door
to tumble in on itself and the sound of heavy

boots or even dogs. I wait. I'm still holding
the light bulb but now with the left hand.

the siren fades. maybe next time they'll barge
in, pull me to the ground and ask me where

I keep the drugs, where the stash of cashews
still in their shells I smuggled into the country

are, did you know that that's illegal? they're
poisonous. they won't know but I'll have a

cyanid capsule embedded in my tooth and bite

down hard. you'll never catch me, I'll say

through the foam. they'll lift off the lamp-
shade, see me and go "we got the wrong guy."

Bottom-Feeder

I woke up wishing there were more
words with z in them. Looking out the
window I imagine myself on the street.
I am on the street. I'm in the middle of
the street and a man stops me and tells
me his name. I never asked for Mr. Alan's
name but I say hello to Mr. Alan and
walk away as my head fills with lead
and the ground feels closer than ever.

The stomach begins to empty. The fish
market is full of fish sleeping in mounds
of ice. They watch as I decide which lucky
one comes home with me. Bivalves. It will
be clams for dinner. Something with less
disdain in its face. They're covered in clay
and so am I and my hands wonder what
it's like living in the sand. The life of a filter.
I step out of my clothes and into the tub. It

fills and then fills with me and I settle at the
bottom wishing I were anything but an
endotherm. I wonder what it's like to filter
and not think. I take in a chest full of bath
and throw up a belly full of clay. I don't get
into bed after this. I put on a pair of socks
and a blazer and go looking for Mr. Alan.
He's wearing a hat that says Chief. I ask

him if he eats shellfish and he walks away.

Quarantine

tapestry filled halls—muffled ears muffle inside
nesting fills you fills your day

whelping plucked and poxed
slivers of paper nestle in the sides

you side-stitch
crossing every pair in a pixel-scene of you and me

nestled in the background
a sense of plus one

Ragman sits in his tiny biohazard suit watching
someone makes a sound it comes from me—my insides speak

the group moves their bodies toward the sound
are they aware of me

am I standing too close or is it the bell's chime
that scatters the herd in a blister of black and magenta

something hollers in the on-lookers
faces pressed against plastic that calls itself glass

the forum looks on as I lecture
writhe free of the topic to describe the skylines massive culture and
        charm

does it sing to you
can you divorce it

or does it pee the bed before the rubber
sheets come in the mail

does the pacemaker beat you into existence or
can you breathe yourself onto the page

we wake in puddles
the mechanic tells you the tune up is suggested but not required

I sit in the waiting room wondering
who dun it   with what

do we section off the house or force feed everyone
until somebody flinches

Apartment Complex

fold me in thirds
press my seams to the floor
stretch me to fit your mattress

the one we found in the neighbors lean-to
half spring and stuffed
half leaves   bramble and
forget-me-nots gone to seed

all skull   skin and scalp
my itch bleeds into the bathwater

the room—a freckled mess with only one door
<toward the exit> <or is it entrance>
with full view of the   toilet

no door but what it has is a seat
the commode   a handle to flush
things my body and yours reject

I tell you I actually liked that meal, it was filling
my body tends to disagree

I sit while you stare at me
looking at my disagreeables turn the stile
and leave the apartment

where do they go?

the east river or
the Harlem
a think tank
or a sardine can in nova scotia

I hope it's the latter
those little guys seeped in oil
fillet'd bellies lain out for the world to see

we should buy them you say
as you carry me from/to the bedroom
that is also the bathroom
that is also our kitchen

buy the lot of them
and cook them up with those turnips
we sowed in Central Park

Ars Poetica

poetry is not like wine
well if it were it would
expire thru the page
perspire onto the table
leaving a ring
and drunkenly set a stain
                      into the carpet
it would sit thick on the tongue
and build up behind the throat
and leave your head thumping
after a long night of indulging

if poetry were wine
it would kiss you hard
after two glasses and soft after three
it'd make getting lost in your own neighborhood
easier and crawling thru the window harder if poetry if

poetry is not like wine
well if it were it would
cause more pregnancies
knock up your daughter
and your wife it wouldn't
get off the babysitter when
                  daddy came home
it would eat all of the good cheese
out the fridge it would make you
late for work and not return your calls

if poetry were wine
it would slap you hard
after two bottles and drive you home
after three it'd tell the police it wasn't drunk
it was late for bingo and its really got to pee if poetry if

poetry is not like wine
baby it's a lot like love
it has you thinking about it in public
it makes you forget the last time
or the first time for that matter
it has you whispering in someone's ear
                    it was a floozy babe
it was out of boredom or lack of trying
it was because it wasn't you in those jeans
If poetry is love then its you
the mountains avalanche and planet's axis tilt it's
my orbit round a brandished star with a crash in
the kitchen it's a fledgling fledged too early
it's kind of like when a pot brownie hits you
in front of company its always pounding
in my ear and running down my leg if poetry if

The Sandwich

A shirt walks into
my daydream it
unfolds itself and as it does

it tells me it hasn't been worn
but could someday, the girl
at the counter hopes today is that day.

she's pregnant but not showing
I'm showing but not pregnant.
she takes a bite of a sandwich

from under the counter. I want it
so desperately I don't care
what kind it is unless it's egg.

she wraps it back
into its foil skin
to fold a pile of denim.

she doesn't see me
leave with the shirt
or the sandwich in toe.

it tastes of soil this sandwich
it turns my mouth into a ceramic pot
rough-sided and baked in the sun.

the shirt is two sizes too big
so we wear it together
while we watch soaps

you call them your stories
which is funny because the stories
never end they get grown out of.

instruction manual

The doctor has me on a regiment

1. Take two large onions, peel them
eat the peels and boil the innards
let the steam pile up behind your eyes
check the mirror for signs of escaping liquid

2. Take three chilis
preferably ones more than one million on the scoville scale
de-vein and seed two of them
place the veiny whites and seeds between the webs of your toes
don socks and shoes applying pressure as needed
apply the remaining flesh of the peppers liberally to the underarms
record any apparent reactions and pop blisters that don't pop themselves
repeat twice a day until desired results are visible
check the mirror for signs of escaping liquid

3. Take one gallon jug of water, drink half
weigh yourself while looking into the mirror
use measuring tape to record the stomachs distention
without turning toward the toilet to relieve yourself
finish the second half of the jug while listening to
the cassette that is included with this instruction manual[1]
press forcibly on the bladder for better results
check the mirror for signs of escaping liquid

4. Take a picture of yourself using the camera on your smartphone
send this photo to someone you find attractive

ask them to tell you which parts of your body
have gone slack in recent months
note the wrinkles along your forehead and the hair round your nipples
Ask them what changes they would make
record the way this makes you feel
remove a pepper from your underarm (applied in step 2) pat your eyes
check the mirror for signs of escaping liquid

1. the pre-recorded sounds of a waterfall in a rainforest

Pear-shaped Diamond

I wish I were you in a trickling necklace
pear-shaped diamond down the back—

she'd tell you I'm run of the mill she'd
wait for you to turn round and keep me for herself

I wonder who's up next is it me or the one who's all leg
smoking something cheap drinking from a plastic cup

their eyes want you I see it they throw you songs
have you doing dances for the record—playing

I want you in all ways that have to do with keeping the lights off
morning being on us through a window of an apartment or a cab

in an alley hiked up a mountain of skin pressure building—
building till there's a new parking lot where our ancestors sleep

Aspen Grove

You told me the time would come
when one of us would leave
I didn't think it'd be me
didn't think it would be tonight—

out of bed and gone like that
you would tell the newspapers
there wasn't even a note that it was
so unlike him to how would you put it

leave with nothing and yet take everything
the fact is I tried to take everything
but it wouldn't fit under my nighty
I tried you first tucking the bedsheet

under your pillowed head
gently rolling you up but it didn't work
your toenails as long as they are
kept catching on the linen pulling

the mattress along with us
I had to put you down and start over—
thought about wrapping you in cellophane
but you tend to sweat easily and profusely

I feared you'd slip out like the cat's
babies did that night on the kitchen rug
he looked at you and cooed—

44

gave you those eyes he always does

out they came all wrapped like sausage
he'd been getting fat that summer we were right
he was your sassy little princess
so much so he sprouted ovaries and a womb—

got knocked up that night he jumped
from the window returning a fearless
worldly woman that had seen it all
I told you I swore I'd seen him in the breezeway

smoking a cigarette one night in late August
but you ignored me—I realized I couldn't take you
at least not all of you in one piece
I went for the kitchen opening the cupboards

the china was far too chatty maybe something
practical that I could use and yet
remember you by be able to rub between my fingers
conjuring tiny moments of you and I together

I found the pail of coffee beans that you had labeled
'beans' and peeled off the lid—the smell raised
bitter pin pricks across my arms
bringing up memories of you and me in winter

oh how it'd make me want to pick up smoking again
hang out the window lighting one
because I wouldn't want the neighbors
seeing me in my nighty on the stoop

you loved it the way the cat loved you
you'd lay around sipping on the sofa
far into the night—you'd wrap
yourself round me patiently

waiting for it to perk you'd watch me
pull it through milk into a tiny cup
I envied your ability to sleep anywhere
at anytime in any position—

I found the cheese your mother sent
from Italy waxed and twined so tight
bulging at the sides—a weightlifter type
all dip tanned and glossy I fought the urge to peel it open

then and there—a liquid halo ripened in a far away land
she rarely sends you anything but I was so desperate
I tucked it under my gown
just like that I am out over the hedge and across

the street before the screen can whip shut—
the house quieting again the long grass
near the thicket wets my legs and thighs
my eyes adjust to see

lights dangling off in the distance—the aspen grove
I wrap your things snug in my nighty
my tightly curled hair unsets while the trees meet me with
outstretched arms and I let them swallow me up

Lightyears

lightyears away there's a little one
letting the pencil rub a dot through
the paper onto a desk into the wood-

grain. you step into the garden to look
up and out lightyears away from the
ground saying sorry into the receiver

sorry that you couldn't tie a necktie
round the moon anymore, that necks
like mine were too thick. the pilot

turns on the plane. I imagine there's
a key in the ignition or a finger trap
that snaps tug and taut. she climbs in

a plane that climbs west claiming the
sky for she, letting her kerchief and
trousers fall into the sea's lip, a waist-

land no one has explored or prodded
around in for years. and lightyears
away another dot is rubbed through

the paper onto a desk into the wood-
grain. petroleum products that buff
it till it shines appear once more

on the surface eons after their first
breath way way before us.

Consumption

I realize that neither of us ever got
what we were looking for in that cup
of soy milk.
>   it fell to the floor in a shadowed
>   clamor soothing floor's stomach from
>   a night of drinking heavy liquor.   your eyelids
>   sway when you're drunk letting your mouth
>   do all the talking about Libra in retrograde and
>   the difference between sour and sweet tamarind.

>   And the soy milk still seeps into the floorboards
>   through the linoleum down and then above
>   the neighbor's head raining into his world of
>   old things he doesn't see anymore they just
>   keep his memories safe and his anxiety at bay.

so consumed he is,
licking his lips in a dream
the soy milk filters off the spackled ceiling stalactites   drip drip
>   drip

>   onto his tongue.

Timetable

We're on a timetable and it's drifting
well, you're drifting. doing anything but
thinking about the trip we're about go on
or how our apartment is sinking.
I want to hear about your day

we're on a time table and it's not comfortable
it's off kilter and I need to sit on a phonebook
to see you on the other side.

I don't even know what kilter means. If I could be one
thing and never have to be anything else I'd

want to be your full time friend
I would be able to lie
or I'd be able to tell you that
there's something after dying
and you'd feel better enough to fall asleep again

and you'd not just stay over anymore
we'd live together.

we're on a timetable and it's about time
everything is about time
all you think about is the end of it. the end of time. but it'll never
be the end of time.

it'll just be the end of you. your body will give up.

or the end of the movie. everyone will get up and leave.
it'll be the end of us. you'll give up on me. all you think about is the
     end.

          what about the nougat middle
        the part where we can't live without each other
     where time slips its shoes off and watches while
       we learn and teach and grow a new language
    a new tongue   no more mouths to feed
just
music and broken in dreams flipping silver dollars through our REMs.

       we're on a timetable and the view is ripe.
stop shaking your leg and peel off your contacts watch everyone else
go by unfiltered.

film noir

off stage a piano is being played off key

there's popcorn being rustled in a bag

the chair your in's springs are creaking

       Faye Dunaway playing me

     playing you in a

  shirtless number   she tells the very real me

I want a meal not a snack

we b-line for the hedges *they look through the hedges toward a window*

       see I told you they were potheads
       they're just like

       you and me   me and me   *their faces aren't there*

waking   nervous-you asks me where my clothes are

the curtain opens and no one is there

          you walk onto the stage in a leather jacket and too much

            oil in your hair   I like it it's slick

you paste a photo to your locker door

        It's me all soaped and sudded up holding a pose

the stage gets all litted up there's me in my knitted nightgown and my
       curlers in

come to bed bucko. I'll switch on your sound machine

      and rub some vicks on your chest   you can't resist a

good old vicks rub   it's the Eucalyptus

the urchin
for PP

everything happens for a reason/he says this and the bubble hangs there
all grey in periods as if there's something to come
it does

I can host/I have cash
it's like playing with play-doh but there isn't any left
just the salt on my fingers

we're living in odd times/the bubble hangs there
and then pops
I don't hear from you for a week and three days

I thumb the picture of you
sewn into my skivvies
I put on a recordput on a shirt   walk downtown

tonight's the night/I feel hands grab for me
as something soaks my pants thru
five hundred dollar bills line my pocket in the morning/there's a train
      and I take it

vick & the gold disk

a symbol of the patriarchy puts his hand up five billion

miles away   It's outside my grasp   I want to shatter its ideals

to pieces

want to put my 3 cents in but can't   she's so far away

Instead I kick the jukebox and our song kicks on it

skips on my favorite note on the bestest line of the chorus but I

don't care   I wriggle

out of my stockings so heavenly thirsting for

it   the dip stick is low but the pistons still fire and the whole

        time

we're waiting for the blip on the screen

                                to download

our pixelated jpeg   our white wedding jizz soak on a pair of

        corduroy

she

voyages away   spirited away   thrown away 40 years ago

with directions on what to say   how to say   and when to hold

your hand up

        we Irish exit   hail a cab   so I can change my

        pants so

                I can smell like rain instead of smelt so

I can kiss the parts of you you can't see   while she looks

        back

snapping our picture in the invert   we're both standing ever so

        ever

        a blue smudge on a long awaited postcard from the future…

54

My left side is my best side

I'm the foster parent of an Australian beer I neither bought
nor wanted, standing over your once lover in a living room none
of us own, cutting his hair while you look on

                                         It's almost

       Halloween

                                  and I'm always in my

       costume

                                  the only day I take it off is

       the 31st

I take off my clothes and leave the party
there's more standing room outside
more space for the clouds to hum

                                  I'm the street lamps coming

       back

                                  on in Harlem—look at them

       shake

I'm telling the truth in fall
colors telling time of year
packing shorts unpacking turtlenecks and knit ties

                                  I'm telling lies to prepare you

       for

                                  him in the stalking grass

       holding

                                        a bubble tea smacking his lips
          after he swallows

he's saying look at them shake
as the clouds hum over my neighborhood
it's like they know there's no space for me here
not anymore

                                        there's plenty in his
          California

                                        plenty in all the places I can't
                                        afford to rent—tumble dry
                                        like the clouds humming
          toward

                                        the East Side
there's a cab waiting to bring me to you
bring me upstairs and unpack
me on that bed with unforgiving springs

                    I'll be your little spoon until at
                    least mid-November or when the
                    heat kicks on… whichever comes first

Nasty

I

you're standing in the corner of the kitchen again you don't know how
          you got there

or what but dad's there   behind you in the backyard there's music
          playing

you hope it's TLC or Janet so you can do all the moves in your
          headspace

I told ya to kneel on those eggshells

you do and they break under your skin they don't break the skin

but they feel like they've dug into your skull   now you can't hear

Thriller starts playing on the boom box   your ears are ringing

you imagine you're walking thru the fog with Michael

you guys have just seen a movie   you're scared but he holds you close

you wonder where someone would come up with kneeling on egg shells

was it on the fly   did they read it in a book   you wish you were older

you want to do a backflip into the future   you
        can't

II

you wake up   your nonna is in front of you   you're
        both far away

she's in a hospital gown with the sheets pulled up with wires and tubes
        attached

she peels an egg in front of you   as she does she tells you about her
        mom

how she was shot by her husband's lover   she was kind

it was at a courthouse   her voice is dry with yoke

your nonna raised her brothers   she had to be stern

there's egg shell on her lip   flecks cover her wrinkled
        fingers

you guys never talk about her son   your father   she
        dies

then he does   you never say goodbye   today in the hospital you do

she says before you go she looks in your eyes and says
          nobody has our eyes just

                              you me and bisnonna

you get in the car   your then boyfriend looks at you
          what

please don't kill me   he drives round the courthouse   he
          doesn't have the time

you break up before you leave for Italy   alone   you don't see any
          of them again

III

you take your headphones off because you thought you heard someone
          yelling

someone next door is dancing   the music's on loud you feel the
          bump it's nice

the music flicks off like the cord came out the wall   something
          large fills the room

the floor boards clap   there's a yell and a whimper in the corner you unplug your headphones   flip on your boom box

the volume's on low so you turn up the dial and press play

Janet says   GIMME A BEAT!   the beat plays at her
          command

you put those yellow gloves back on and start dancing
          stop for a sec

turn the boom box toward the wall   you wish you could find your
          tap shoes

wish you had a louder stereo   she goes OH YOU NASTY BOYS!

there are eggs in the fridge   you take one out and crack it
          into the pan

instead of a three pointer into the rubbish can half the egg slips under
          the fridge

the next week you empty the apartment   fill a uhaul
          leave the egg

change your address   change your underwear
          phone a friend

Ruckus Pie Recipe

the hubbard squash sits all
robin egg all I'm fragile but
I can take a fall
and I do I fall

for strange stars I don't recall
and songs I haven't heard
laughs on the subway
and we're the only ones there
I fall
and the hubbard sings for us too

on the pavement and the driveway
from the second floor of the barn we sing
to her and she shows us innard gifts of
orange and seed
pulp—she'll make a good soup

neighbors see us and they
yell about the ruckus

Eggs

There are eggs on the pillow again
still warm still calcifying since late

last night. Eggs that came before them
were fried or whipped into peaks but,

not these eggs. I lay my head gently to
them, keep them company by reading

the paper and singing along with the
radio. They growth spurt filling their

igloos and thatch-roofed houses restless

I take them to the library to stretch
out in the stacks. chaucer turns to

milton turns to angelou and frost
and the whole time I wonder if they

absorb what I do. I lay my head on
the pillow.

What a thing to be sown to someone
through thought and mind, the silk-

worms spin us connect us whisked
onto to the lighthouse onto making

of Americans uttering into eggs I no
longer have to read to they're reading

on their own, the hours passing
the bricks falling shells cracking blood

puttering through hollow bone and
rib until the stacks lay empty the bed

unfurls and the lightbulb on the bed-
side lamp has gone out and the eggs

I see everyday are now fowl of all type
in the garden necking or the city park

swinging and chatting about a new
book they read that has to do with
being visible and seeing your reflection
in a mug of soup in the muddy stamps

on the hallway floor that when you
follow them lead to a classroom filled

with empty chairs a basket could be
there filled with eggs you could lay

your head on listen and hear a story.

New Years Day

two Conway boys in toilet paper jackets on New Years Day.
                    sissy kid. delicate. we were a match. book of
        matches.
                            they made fun of you too. a voice all
        crackly crispy like
        mine.
        we play a nasty game of tag while the other kids refuse to play
        along.
                            you ask me if the water's cold. if it'd
        break us in two—

                                            floaters
                                                they want
        my swan song to play

                                                want my
        earrings pulled out by gulls

                                                while the
        tide knots and pulls.
                                        bobbers
                                            I want to be
        folded again.

                                            lick the
        envelope and crawl ever so

                                            closer to the
        sea floor. let me.
                                        allow me to sleep
        there.

                                            let all my air out and

wait. listening.

sound travels faster in water. so much faster. I read that in a book about
    sperm whales.
                                            I won't open my
    mouth anymore.

            I can't feel you, you say. this straight voice
                            like there are people around.
        your hands feel for me but all you're getting is this
    ball of eels.

                        the boardwalk empties. we
    empty.
            we go local. then express ourselves while we
    itch our sand fleas.
            I hold your hand. you tell me what
    you were thinking
                    under those waves.
            I learn from a man in a top hat about rigging
    your metro card
            so that you can ride free forever.
            It works and now I'm a criminal. I don't feel
    any different.
            that year we wore Coney Island as a
    skin.

close to the heart

you play things
close to the chest
you let nothing in
or anything go for that matter
you're cell membrane ameba
walking crawling on all hairs you're a
hairless cat in winter bundled up to the
pill you're pulling out your hair when
I'm not around you're laughing at all
their jokes in your stranger laugh
you're telling everyone you ate
today you're holding out a hand not
to be pulled close but to push them
away you're not like the others
you're holding me close at night so
close our breathing is in rhythm our
eyes flutter in REM to the same
snare our bodies start to smell
the same think the same shit the same
our iPods sync the same songs
our tickets read the same gate
the same destination we get on the
same train we get on the same
flight we tell the same stories to
different friends we laugh in the
laugh we use when we're alone together
when the fire goes out and
the last log turns and the mountain

aches under the snow the same
snow that paints the cabin we sit in
the same cabin someone else
stayed in yesterday hopefully not
the same sheets but we're too tired
to check for bed bugs too tired to
open the wardrobe too tired to think
about anything but the
breathing and the present and the
way we fed each other clams in
the restaurant the same way we
think about food and how it
consumes the parts of our day we
want to live for ourselves but
don't how electric November feels
compared to October how we are
turning to charcoal like the fire is
while we sleep like the charcoal
footprints we followed out the
bedroom and into the hallway the
one's that patted down the stairs
that all of us take our shoes off
before we climb before we
enter the space we all share with the
roommate you never see and I can't
for the life of me remember
his name we only remember
his coughs—coughed out soot
into the bath at night into the early
morning with the shower on for
hours on end

or better when we go to see the
elephants in the Bronx
their ears like mine
mine all flappy
big enough for the both of us
to fly away and leave
call a new place
home could be Elmhurst
could be Jackson Heights could be
a run down rent control on the UWS
could be anything as long as
I'm with you laying on our bed
telling each other the dreams
we'd freshly had
before they're erased and gone
right before you put your eyes in
and tell me a story
in the shower mist

Glowworm

that spittle beaded up along its lip
hangs   an apostrophe alone
floats upon a saline sea of sorts

a sea of the dead—skin cells that
passed their expiration days ago
sloughed   stranded on the street

while newborns split walling you off from me
everything in the neighborhood aligns
taking sides—yours   always yours

I'm always the other   running
the write-in vote miss congeniality
can't keep my mouth closed   the fool they say   the fool!

their eyes don't fool   I walk through that beaded curtain
rub passed   dangle back into place
again in free flow hanging against you   the clatter

Since February

as months pass
the things you
purchased

the food stuff
and books of stamps

have gotten used up

their wrappings
and packaging

tossed away

their innards went in me
or onto canvas

the photo albums
fill with him and others

while you sit down river
tossing in and out

of my dreams

while the nights fill with
lonesome mockingbird
songs

and dried up
mandarine rinds
on the nightstand

Winter solstice and then August

whiff the back of your shirt deep
fibers bleached with sunscreen
little spoon

your dreams have you waiting in
line

have you selling bags of peanuts
with me on the pier

tell me it's going to be wonderful

Antonio Addessi is a poet and writer living in New York City. He received his BA in English from the University of Maine('15) and his MFA in Creative Writing Poetry from Columbia University('20). His poems "old ironsides" and "fish and the creel" were first published digitally by Wrath-Bearing Tree.

Printed in the USA
CPSIA information can be obtained
at www.ICGtesting.com
LVHW090113070324
773789LV00031B/890

9 781608 642007